CHANITA R. RAMSEY

I Choose Me: Thriving in Singleness God's Way

Bootcamp Edition

INSPIRED
BY LOVE & GRACE
PUBLISHING

Second edition

ISBN: 978-1-970671-01-8

This book was professionally typeset on Reedsy.
Find out more at reedsy.com

Dedication

To the woman who has carried heartbreak, betrayal, and disappointment.
To the soul who has walked through seasons of toxicity,
endured love that cut deeper than it healed, and questioned whether she would ever
be enough.
May these pages meet you where you are
and guide you toward the freedom God has waiting for you.
To the woman discovering that her wholeness is her greatest superpower,
and that when she chooses herself, she activates the life God intended her to live.

Contents

Acknowledgments

There comes a moment when a woman finally exhales—the moment she realizes that the pieces she thought were broken were actually becoming something beautiful. I Choose Me was born from that exhale.

To every woman who has walked through heartbreak, betrayal, and disappointment—your story matters. The pain that once tried to destroy you is the very soil God is using to grow you. You are not defined by what hurt you, but by how you rise from it.

To the one who has endured toxic love, questioned her worth, and felt unseen—may these pages remind you that you were never forgotten. God has been rewriting your story all along.

And to the woman standing in her season of singleness—please hear this truth: you are not waiting to be chosen. You already are. This is your becoming season.

My heart overflows with gratitude for my sister in Christ, **Patrina**. Thank you for being my intercessor when I had no words, my encourager when I had no strength, and my mirror when I couldn't see my own reflection. I am forever thankful for your presence in my journey.

May this acknowledgment serve as a gentle whisper to every woman reading: *you are worthy, you are whole, and your healing is your victory.* Choosing yourself is not pride—it's peace.

With love and gratitude,

—Chanita R. Ramsey

Introduction

There comes a moment in every woman's life when enough is enough. Maybe you've felt it too—broken, used, overlooked, and utterly exhausted. Exhausted from proving your worth through the eyes of others, exhausted from giving your heart to those who didn't value it, exhausted from believing the lie that your single season means something is wrong with you.

And then it hits—you say it out loud: **"Enough. I choose me."**

This is your turning point. A moment of clarity where you realize that being single is not a curse—it is your classroom. A sacred space where God is shaping, refining, and preparing you to step into the fullness of who He created you to be. This is not about waiting for someone else to make you whole. It's about claiming your own wholeness and refusing to settle for anything less than the life God intended for you.

This workbook is different. It's raw. It's real. It's interactive. You won't just read words—you will **do the work**: confront the lies, face the patterns, wrestle with your heart, and rise stronger than ever.

You will:

- Encounter **truths that sting but heal**.
- Gain **tools** to grow spiritually, emotionally, and mentally.
- Receive **empowerment** to choose yourself boldly, without apology.

You will not:

- Be told your pain was easy or deserved.
- Get a quick fix or formula for "perfect love."
- Be coddled with sugar-coated platitudes.

This workbook is designed to meet you where you are and **take you higher**—to a place where your single season becomes a sacred space, a divine classroom, and a powerful preparation for everything God has planned for you.

The Challenge

Here's the truth: this journey will confront you. You may face hard realities about your past, your habits, and even your current thinking. You might feel uncomfortable, defensive, or emotional. That's normal—it means the Holy Spirit is at work.

Do not give up. Do not quit halfway.

Push through. Let the exercises, reflections, and challenges **stir your heart**. Let the Holy Spirit reveal what needs to be healed, reshaped, or released. The discomfort is the doorway to transformation.

Your challenge for this introduction is simple but powerful:

Write down one truth about yourself that you have been avoiding.

- Don't judge it.
- Don't try to fix it yet.
- Just name it, bring it to God, and commit to exploring it fully during this workbook journey.

How to Use This Workbook

- **12-Week Journey:** Each week focuses on a core theme.
- **Daily Micro-Challenges:** Optional exercises, reflections, prayers, and actions to keep you engaged every day.
- **Solo or Group-Friendly:** Complete it on your own or in a study group for accountability.
- **Action + Reflection:** You will not just read—you will **do the work**, confront your patterns, and claim your wholeness.
- If you are ready to stop surviving and start thriving, if you are ready to

choose you, then this workbook is your road map.

It will be raw.
  It will be real.
  It will be transformational.
  Welcome to **the breaking point**.
  Welcome to **your awakening**.
  Welcome to **choosing you**.

I

Part One: The Reality of Singleness

Week 1 : Conditioned to Crave

Core Lesson

From childhood, society teaches us that **happiness and worth are tied to being loved by someone else**. Dolls, fairy tales, Disney movies, and even church messaging often communicate: *You're only enough when a man validates you.*

As a result, many women chase approval, attention, or love, believing it will complete them. This leaves a hollow ache when relationships fail, or when your "happiness" depends on someone else's presence.

Here's the truth:

- Chasing approval leads to poor decisions and settling for less than God's best.
- Your single season is a classroom for growth, clarity, and alignment with God.
- Wholeness is spiritual armor—it protects your heart, mind, and purpose until the right love, if God allows it, enters your life.

You are whole. You are enough. **God created you complete before anyone else enters your life.** Recognizing this is the first step toward breaking cycles of seeking external validation.

Tough Love Reality Check

- Ask yourself: How often have you **given away your time, affection, or even your body** to feel seen or loved?
- Truth: Repeatedly seeking validation outside of God **leaves you empty, frustrated, and misaligned with your purpose**.
- Healing starts when you **face this conditioning and take responsibility for reclaiming your worth**.

Real-Life Scenario

Kayla, 27, spent years chasing approval. She dated men who were convenient, exciting, or emotionally unavailable. Each time, she hoped for fulfillment but ended up with emptiness.

Through journaling, setting boundaries, and leaning into God's truth, Kayla discovered: **her value wasn't dependent on anyone else**. Her single season became a classroom, teaching self-respect, spiritual alignment, and emotional resilience.

Reflection Questions

1. Write about a time you felt "less than" because you were single.
2. What messages—family, media, friends, church—shaped your belief that you needed someone else to be whole?
3. In what areas do you still seek external validation instead of God's truth?
4. How would your life feel if you fully embraced that you are already whole?

Raw Teaching Exercise

- List **5 lies** you believed about your worth due to cultural, familial, or media messaging.
- Beside each, write the **truth from God's Word** that counters it.

Commitment Challenge

Declare:

"I will stop seeking my worth in the eyes of others. I choose to see myself as God sees me: whole, valuable, and enough."

Action Steps

1. List **3 ways** you've sought validation outside of God.
2. Identify **one behavior or thought pattern** you will stop immediately.
3. Set a **daily reminder** to recite your affirmation and reinforce your worth in God.

Accountability Challenge

- Share your commitment with a trusted friend, mentor, or small group.
- Ask them to **check in weekly** on your progress.
- Journal your insights: what's working, what's challenging, and what you're learning.

Scripture Anchor

- **Psalm 139:14** – *"I praise you because I am fearfully and wonderfully made; your works are wonderful, I know that full well."*
- **Galatians 1:10** – *"Am I now trying to win the approval of human beings, or of God? Or am I trying to please people? If I were still trying to please people, I would not be a servant of Christ."*

Prayer & Affirmation

Prayer:

"Lord, help me see myself through Your eyes. Heal the wounds caused by lies about my worth. Teach me to find validation, peace, and joy in You. I surrender my need for approval to You and claim my wholeness."

Affirmation:

I am whole. I am enough. I am not defined by my relationship status. I choose God's truth over the opinions of others.

Daily Micro-Challenges

Day 1 – Core Lesson & Reflections

- Read the core lesson.
- Journal: Identify one way you've sought external validation.

Day 2 – Tough Love Reality Check

- Reflect on the last time you compromised your peace for attention.
- Journal: What did it cost you spiritually, emotionally, or mentally?

Day 3 – Real-Life Scenario & Reflection

- Read Kayla's story.
- Write a parallel experience from your own life.

Day 4 – Commitment Challenge & Action Step

- Declare your commitment.
- Identify one behavior or thought pattern to stop immediately.

Day 5 – Accountability Challenge

- Share your declaration with someone trustworthy.
- Check in about progress or struggles.

Day 6 – Scripture Meditation

- Meditate on Psalm 139:14 and Galatians 1:10.
- Journal how these scriptures affirm your worth.

Day 7 – Reflection, Prayer & Affirmation

- Review and answer reflection questions.
- Complete the Raw Teaching Exercise.
- Pray and speak your affirmation aloud.
- Reflect on any changes in mindset or emotions.

End-of-Week Quiz

1. True or False: My worth depends on someone noticing or loving me.
2. List two cultural or social messages you've internalized about singleness.
3. Identify one lie you believed about your worth and the truth from God that counters it.
4. How could embracing your wholeness today change your future relationships?
5. Name one concrete action you will take this week to reinforce your wholeness.

End-of-Week Challenge – The Wholeness Challenge

Choose one area where you've been seeking validation from others (social media, past relationships, friendships). For the next 7 days:

- Track your thoughts and feelings each time that craving arises.
- Pause, pray, and remind yourself: *I am whole. God has made me complete.*

Journal nightly about how practicing this awareness impacts your mindset, decisions, and confidence.

Week 2: Nights That Hit Different

Core Lesson

Some nights, your body doesn't just want love—it **demands it**. Your spirit says, *wait, trust, pray*, but your flesh whispers, *just this once, it won't hurt.* And so the struggle begins.

Late at night, when the world is quiet and your heart is loud, temptation shows up in texts, DMs, or even memories of past relationships. Your mind says, *Maybe this time it will be different.* Your body convinces you it will satisfy the emptiness.

The truth: giving in doesn't satisfy—it **amplifies the hunger**. One fleeting moment, one text you shouldn't have sent, one compromise, and the emptiness grows. The craving doesn't vanish—it multiplies.

Your **body is not the enemy**—it's a tool. Master it, don't let it master you. Your spirit longs for fullness that only comes from God, not temporary pleasure or validation.

Tough Love Reality Check

- Temptation will always arrive—often at the worst possible times.
- Giving in may feel good momentarily but **leaves your spirit drained, your heart hollow, and your glow dimmed**.
- Mastering your flesh is not optional. **Your peace, clarity, and future happiness depend on it.**

Real-Life Scenario

The Late-Night Text:
It's 2:17 a.m. Your phone buzzes. He's someone you know isn't right for you. Loneliness grips you. You've waited long enough. He makes you feel desired. You start typing a message, delete, pause, type again. By morning, your soul feels heavy, your heart hollow, and the craving stronger than before.

Going Through the Motions:
You're exhausted, alone, and aching. You convince yourself it's harmless. You seek comfort in touch or fantasy. Afterwards, you feel drained and frustrated. The craving comes back louder next time.

Soul Ties:
Every compromise leaves a piece of your heart tangled in someone else's hands. These connections linger, cloud your clarity, and dim your glow.

Reflection Questions

1. When does temptation hit you hardest—time of day, emotional state, or situation?
2. How does feeding the flesh temporarily make you feel, and what are the long-term effects?
3. Who or what triggers your cravings, and what boundaries can you put in place?
4. How can you redirect your desire toward spiritual fulfillment instead of temporary escape?

Journaling Prompts

- Write about the last time you gave in to a fleeting desire. How did it affect your spirit the next day?
- List the situations, people, or places that most often test your discipline. How can you remove or manage them?
- Describe what your life would look like if your body and spirit were

aligned, and temptation no longer controlled you.

Commitment Challenge

Declare:

"I will not give in to temporary pleasure. I choose to honor my body, protect my heart, and trust God's timing for fulfillment."

Action Steps

1. Identify the **triggers** that lead you to compromise your boundaries.
2. List **3 ways** you will protect yourself from giving in to temptation.
3. Set up a **daily reminder** to pray and affirm your worth and self-control.

Accountability Challenge

- Share your commitment with a trusted friend or mentor.
- Ask them to **check in with you** once a week about struggles and progress.
- Journal weekly insights: what worked, what tempted you, and how God helped you resist.

Scripture Anchor

- **1 Corinthians 6:19-20** – *"Do you not know that your bodies are temples of the Holy Spirit, who is in you... Therefore honor God with your bodies."*
- **Galatians 5:16** – *"So I say, walk by the Spirit, and you will not gratify the desires of the flesh."*

Prayer & Affirmation

Prayer:

"Lord, help me master my flesh before it masters me. Give me clarity, strength, and courage to choose You over temptation. Protect my heart, guard my mind, and guide my body to honor You."

Affirmation:

I am not a slave to desire. I am whole. I am disciplined. I honor my body, my spirit, and my worth above temporary escape.

Daily Micro-Challenges

Day 1 – Core Lesson & Reflection:

- Read the core lesson.
- Journal: Identify your **top 3 triggers** for late-night temptation.

Day 2 – Tough Love Reality Check:

- Reflect: When did you last give in, and how did it affect you spiritually or emotionally?
- Journal the **consequences** of giving in.

Day 3 – Real-Life Scenario & Reflection:

- Read the scenarios above.
- Write your own experience and feelings in a parallel situation.

Day 4 – Commitment Challenge & Action Step:

- Declare your commitment.
- Take **one practical step** today to avoid temptation (delete contact, block, set boundaries).

Day 5 – Accountability Challenge:

- Share your commitment with a trusted friend or mentor.

- Discuss your **progress and struggles**.

Day 6 – Scripture Meditation:

- Meditate on **1 Corinthians 6:19-20** and **Galatians 5:16**.
- Journal how these verses empower you to resist temptation.

Day 7 – Reflection, Prayer & Affirmation:

- Answer reflection questions.
- Complete journaling prompts.
- Pray and speak your affirmation aloud.
- Note any changes in mindset, emotions, or self-control.

End-of-Week Quiz

1. True or False: Giving in to temptation brings lasting fulfillment.
2. List **3 triggers** that challenge your discipline.
3. What steps can you take to master your flesh in moments of weakness?
4. How does aligning your body and spirit strengthen your wholeness?
5. Identify one scripture that reminds you of your self-control and worth.

End-of-Week Challenge – The Self-Control Challenge

For the next 7 days:

- Track each moment temptation arises.
- Pause, pray, and speak: *I am disciplined. I honor God with my body and spirit.*
- Journal nightly about the **impact on your mindset, decisions, and spiritual growth**.

Week 3 – Mr. Right Now vs. Mr. Wrong Everything

Core Lesson

Some men are convenient. They are available on your timeline, show up when it's easy, and make you feel noticed—but they **aren't ready for a real relationship**. Some men are dangerous to your peace, promising excitement, thrill, and connection, but leaving destruction in their wake.

In your journey, you may encounter three types of men:

- **Mr. Right Now:** Exciting, convenient, emotionally unavailable. Wants your time, attention, or body—but not your heart.
- **Mr. Wrong Everything:** Pulls you into chaos, repeats patterns of deceit, neglect, or disrespect. Drains your peace and dims your glow.
- **Mr. Right (God-Ordained):** Adds to your life, aligns with your values, and propels you toward your God-given purpose. He honors your heart and protects your peace.

Too often, women chase **Mr. Right Now** or tolerate **Mr. Wrong Everything**, mistaking temporary attention for love. Your single season is a **classroom to recognize patterns, set boundaries, and cultivate discernment**.

Tough Love Reality Check

- Repeating the same type of relationships keeps you trapped in cycles of **half-love, heartbreak, and soul ties**.
- Validation from the wrong people is **temporary**; it never fills the void.
- **Your peace and future relationships** depend on recognizing the difference between convenience, chaos, and God's best.

Real-Life Scenario

The Late-Night Text:

It's 11:45 p.m. Your phone buzzes. He's Mr. Right Now—fun, exciting, unavailable emotionally. You text, hoping for connection. You feel alive for a moment, but by morning, the guilt, emptiness, and shame return.

The Drama Cycle:

Mr. Wrong Everything shows up, promising attention and thrill. You chase, compromise boundaries, and try to fix him. The pattern repeats. Chaos ensues, leaving your spirit bruised and your clarity clouded.

The God-Ordained Choice:

Mr. Right arrives aligned with your values, life purpose, and God's timing. He honors your heart, supports your growth, and protects your peace. This is the love worth waiting for.

Reflection Questions

1. What patterns do I see in the men I choose?
2. Have I repeatedly chosen excitement over peace or convenience over God's best?
3. Where have I compromised my values or peace for temporary attention or thrill?
4. How would prioritizing God's love and timing change my romantic choices?

Journaling Prompts

- Write about the last time you were drawn to Mr. Right Now or tolerated Mr. Wrong Everything. How did it make you feel during and after?
- Reflect on recurring types: what **unhealed wounds or unmet needs** are influencing your choices?
- Describe **Mr. Right** as God sees him. What traits, behaviors, and alignment with purpose does he have?

Commitment Challenge

Declare:

"I will no longer settle for convenience or chaos. I choose God's best. I protect my heart, honor my peace, and wait for the love that aligns with His plan."

Action Steps

1. **Name the Pattern:** Write down the types of men you repeatedly fall for and the behaviors that keep you trapped.
2. **Set Boundaries:** No late-night texts, hookups, or emotional compromises. Protect your peace.
3. **Cut Soul Ties:** Forgive, release, and pray for freedom from lingering emotional connections.
4. **Protect Your Glow:** Engage in practices that uplift you—journaling, prayer, fitness, or spiritual study.

Accountability Challenge

- Share your commitment with a trusted friend, mentor, or small group.
- Check in weekly about temptations, emotional triggers, and growth.
- Journal insights: what's working, what's challenging, and how God is shaping your discernment.

Scripture Anchor

- **Proverbs 4:23** – *"Above all else, guard your heart, for everything you do flows from it."*
- **Psalm 37:4** – *"Take delight in the Lord, and he will give you the desires of your heart."*

Prayer & Affirmation

Prayer:

"Lord, help me recognize who is right for my heart and who is not. Protect me from temptation, compromise, and heartbreak. Teach me patience, discernment, and trust in Your timing for love."

Affirmation:

I am not an option; I am the prize. I protect my heart, honor my peace, and trust God to guide me into the love He has prepared.

Daily Micro-Challenges

Day 1 – Core Lesson & Reflection:

- Read the core lesson.
- Journal: Identify recurring patterns in your past relationships.

Day 2 – Tough Love Reality Check:

- Reflect: When did you compromise your peace for attention?
- Journal how it affected your heart, spirit, and clarity.

Day 3 – Real-Life Scenario & Reflection:

- Read scenarios above.

- Write a parallel experience and what you learned about your choices.

Day 4 – Commitment Challenge & Action Step:

- Declare your commitment.
- Take **one step** today to avoid temptation or chaotic relationships.

Day 5 – Accountability Challenge:

- Share your commitment with a trusted person.
- Discuss temptations and triggers from the week.

Day 6 – Scripture Meditation:

- Meditate on **Proverbs 4:23** and **Psalm 37:4**.
- Journal how these verses empower your discernment.

Day 7 – Reflection, Prayer & Affirmation:

- Answer reflection questions.
- Complete journaling prompts.
- Pray and speak your affirmation aloud.
- Note changes in mindset, emotional clarity, or self-control.

End-of-Week Quiz

1. True or False: Mr. Right Now respects my heart and values.
2. Name one way Mr. Wrong Everything drains your peace.
3. How can identifying patterns in your choices protect your heart?
4. Describe one trait of Mr. Right aligned with God's plan for your life.
5. What is one concrete step you will take this week to protect your heart?

End-of-Week Challenge – The Discernment Challenge

For the next 7 days:

- Track thoughts and feelings when tempted to chase Mr. Right Now or tolerate Mr. Wrong Everything.
- Pause, pray, and speak: *I will wait for God's best. I honor my heart, my peace, and my purpose.*
- Journal nightly about how this awareness impacts your choices, mindset, and emotional clarity.

Week 4 – The Loneliness That Eats You Alive

Core Lesson

L oneliness can hit harder at night, in quiet moments, or when social media reminds you that others are living, loving, and thriving. The ache whispers lies: *"You're behind. You're missing out. You're not enough."*

Many turn to temporary fixes—food, shopping, social media, late-night hookups, or overworking—to numb the emptiness. But these only **mask the pain**, leaving it louder and unhealed.

Your single season is **a spiritual training ground**: a chance to face your heart, confront unhealed wounds, and build resilience. God calls you to **embrace your wholeness**, even in the moments when loneliness threatens to define you.

Tough Love Reality Check

- Numbing your pain doesn't erase it—it **magnifies it**.
- Temporary fixes steal your clarity, joy, and God-given peace.
- Ignoring the ache delays healing, self-discovery, and preparation for true love.
- Facing loneliness is **not weakness**; it's courage.

Real-Life Scenario

One night, you scroll endlessly through social media. Every couple's photo, engagement post, and romantic getaway fuels the ache inside. You order takeout you don't want, spend money unnecessarily, and tell yourself it's just "treating yourself." But inside, you cry silently, wondering: *Will I ever feel seen, loved, or whole?*

That night, you realize: **numbing the pain only buries it deeper**. Healing begins when you **face your loneliness instead of running from it**.

Reflection Questions

1. Where do you turn when loneliness hits hardest? Food, shopping, scrolling, hookups, or work?
2. How do these numbing habits affect your heart, mind, and spirit in the long run?
3. What truths about your worth are you avoiding by distracting yourself?
4. How might your life change if you faced loneliness instead of hiding from it?

Journaling Prompts

- List the numbing habits you use when lonely. How effective are they really?
- Write about a night you cried alone. What were the real emotions underneath?
- Imagine a safe, healing space for yourself. What does it look like? Who or what supports you there?

Commitment Challenge

Declare:

"I will not let loneliness define me. I will face my pain, seek God's comfort, and choose healing over temporary fixes."

Action Steps

1. **Acknowledge the Pain:** Name your emotions—sadness, longing, anger, or fear. Awareness is the first step to healing.
2. **Remove Toxic Triggers:** Limit social media scrolling, avoid comparison-inducing content, and create boundaries that protect your mental and emotional space.
3. **Create Safe Spaces:** Spend time in environments that nurture your soul—prayer, journaling, nature, or trusted friends.
4. **Replace Numbing with Nourishing:**

- Food → mindful cooking or healthy nutrition
- Shopping → saving, organizing, giving to others
- Scrolling → journaling, reading, or scripture study
- Hookups → physical activity, creative work, or prayer

1. **Reach Out:** Call a friend, mentor, or support group. Share your heart with someone who can walk with you through the ache.
2. **Prayer & Surrender:** Hand over the loneliness to God and invite Him to **comfort, heal, and guide** you.

Accountability Challenge

- Share your commitment with a trusted friend or small group.
- Check in midweek and at the end of the week about progress, struggles, and insights.
- Journal: what triggers arose, what practices helped, and what you learned

about yourself and God's presence.

Scripture Anchor

- **Psalm 34:18** – *"The Lord is close to the brokenhearted and saves those who are crushed in spirit."*
- **Isaiah 41:10** – *"So do not fear, for I am with you; do not be dismayed, for I am your God. I will strengthen you and help you; I will uphold you with my righteous right hand."*

Prayer & Affirmation

Prayer:

"Lord, help me face my loneliness instead of hiding from it. Heal the emptiness in my heart and teach me to find joy, purpose, and peace in You. Protect me from numbing habits that steal my clarity and glow. Surround me with safe people, safe spaces, and Your love."

Affirmation:

I will not allow loneliness to define me. I am whole, I am worthy, and I am loved by God. My worth is found in Him, not in distractions or temporary fixes.

Daily Micro-Challenges

Day 1 – Core Lesson & Reflection:

- Read the core lesson.
- Journal: Identify your top 3 numbing habits and why you turn to them.

Day 2 – Tough Love Reality Check:

- Reflect on a night you used a numbing habit to avoid loneliness.
- Journal how it affected your spirit, clarity, and emotional well-being.

Day 3 – Real-Life Scenario & Reflection:

- Read the scenario above.
- Write about a similar experience and how it impacted your decisions.

Day 4 – Commitment Challenge & Action Step:

- Declare your commitment aloud.
- Take **one action** today to replace a numbing habit with a nourishing habit.

Day 5 – Accountability Challenge:

- Share your commitment with someone you trust.
- Discuss what worked and what was challenging so far.

Day 6 – Scripture Meditation:

- Meditate on **Psalm 34:18** and **Isaiah 41:10**.
- Journal how these verses bring comfort, strength, and clarity.

Day 7 – Reflection, Prayer & Affirmation:

- Answer reflection questions.
- Journal insights, breakthroughs, or emotions faced this week.
- Pray and speak your affirmation aloud.
- Reflect on changes in mindset, confidence, and self-worth.

End-of-Week Quiz

1. True or False: Numbing habits erase loneliness.
2. List two numbing habits you've used to distract from pain.
3. What is the long-term effect of avoiding loneliness instead of facing it?

4. How can creating safe spaces help you process emotions?
5. Name one nourishing habit you will implement next week to replace a numbing habit.

End-of-Week Challenge – The Healing Challenge

For the next 7 days:

- Track when loneliness hits. Pause, pray, and speak: *I am whole. I am loved. God is with me.*
- Swap **one numbing habit** per day with a nourishing habit (journal, walk, scripture, creative outlet).

Journal nightly: How did replacing the numbing habit affect your mood, choices, and mindset?

II

Part Two: Healing & Wholeness

Week 5 – When God Steps Into Your Mess

Core Lesson

S ometimes life smashes you against reality. You think you're in control, making your own choices, and suddenly—bam—the consequences hit: broken relationships, unmet expectations, heartbreak, and regret. That's when God steps in—not in judgment, but in love.

Your mess is **not punishment**. Every mistake, heartbreak, and disappointment is a signpost guiding you toward God's love, presence, and restoration.

Surrender doesn't feel comfortable. It never feels convenient. But surrender is freedom, and when you let God step into your mess, He shows you a life you could never achieve on your own.

Tough Love Reality Check

- God doesn't enjoy watching you struggle—He waits until brokenness wakes you up.
- The pain exposes what you've been choosing over Him: people, habits, distractions.
- Your mess is a **wake-up call**, not a dead end.
- Resistance, fear, and discomfort are normal, but they don't nullify God's plan for your restoration.

Real-Life Scenario

I spent years chasing what I thought would make me happy—relationships that promised love, validation from friends, and approval from the world. Every choice seemed right in the moment, but left me empty by morning.

One night, exhausted and broken, God whispered to me: *"Choose Me, for I love you with an everlasting love. I have always loved you—in spite of you choosing other things, you have always been My choice."*

In that moment, I surrendered. My pride resisted. My flesh panicked. But surrender wasn't weakness—it was **freedom**. God met me in my mess and showed me a peace I had never known.

Reflection Questions

1. What areas of your life feel messy, broken, or out of control right now?
2. How have your choices led you away from God's plan, and what wake-up signs has He placed in your life?
3. What fears or resistance come up when you think about surrendering fully to God?
4. How might surrender, even when uncomfortable, lead to freedom in your life?

Journaling Prompts

- Write about a moment when God whispered to your spirit. What did He say, and how did it feel?
- Reflect on a choice that led to heartbreak or emptiness. How could surrender to God have changed the outcome?
- Describe what freedom would look like if you fully let God step into your mess.

Commitment & Action Steps

1. **Acknowledge the Mess** – Be honest about the areas of your life that are broken or out of control.
2. **Invite God In** – Speak to Him openly; He is always present.
3. **Release Control** – Stop trying to fix, manipulate, or force outcomes.
4. **Seek Presence Over Approval** – Focus on being with God, not pleasing people or circumstances.
5. **Trust the Process** – Healing and freedom take time, but God is faithful.

Commitment Challenge:
"I surrender my life, my heart, and my will to God. I will let Him step into my mess and lead me to freedom and restoration."

Accountability Challenge

- Share your commitment with a trusted friend, mentor, or small group.
- Check in weekly to discuss progress, fears, and breakthroughs.
- Journal accountability insights: what's working, what's challenging, and what you're learning.

Scripture Anchor

- Psalms 34:18 – *"The Lord is close to the brokenhearted and saves those who are crushed in spirit."*
- Isaiah 61:3 – *"...to give them a crown of beauty instead of ashes, the oil of joy instead of mourning, and a garment of praise instead of a spirit of despair."*

Prayer & Affirmation

Prayer:
"Lord, I surrender my mess to You. I release the choices I've made that have hurt me and those I love. Come into the broken places of my heart and fill

them with Your love, peace, and purpose. Teach me to trust You even when surrender doesn't feel comfortable. Restore my spirit and guide me into Your freedom. Amen."

Affirmation:

I am not defined by my mistakes, heartbreak, or mess. God's love is everlasting. I surrender my life, heart, and will to Him. In my brokenness, I find freedom, restoration, and wholeness.

Daily Micro-Challenges

Day 1 – Core Lesson & Reflection:

- Read the core lesson.
- Journal: Identify areas of your life that feel messy or broken.

Day 2 – Tough Love Reality Check:

- Reflect on the wake-up calls God has sent in your life.
- Journal: How has brokenness pointed you toward Him?

Day 3 – Real-Life Scenario Reflection:

- Read the story.
- Journal: Recall a moment when God whispered to your spirit.

Day 4 – Commitment Challenge & Action Step:

- Declare your surrender aloud.
- Identify one area where you need to release control to God.

Day 5 – Accountability Challenge:

- Share your commitment with a trusted person.
- Check in and discuss fears or breakthroughs.

Day 6 – Scripture Meditation:

- Meditate on Psalms 34:18 and Isaiah 61:3.
- Journal how these scriptures affirm God's nearness in your brokenness.

Day 7 – Reflection, Prayer & Affirmation:

- Answer reflection questions and journaling prompts.
- Pray and speak your affirmation aloud.
- Reflect on any mindset or emotional shifts over the week.

End-of-Week Quiz

1. True or False: God only loves me when I make the right choices.
2. Identify one area of your life where God is calling you to surrender.
3. Write about a wake-up call God has sent you and what it revealed.
4. How might surrendering fully to God change the outcome of your current struggles?
5. Name one concrete action you will take this week to invite God into your mess.

End-of-Week Challenge – The Surrender Challenge

For the next 7 days:

- Each time you feel overwhelmed by brokenness or chaos, pause and say: *"Lord, I surrender this to You."*
- Journal nightly about how surrender impacted your decisions, peace, and clarity.

Celebrate small victories as God works through your mess to bring freedom, restoration, and wholeness.

Week 6 – The Glow-Up From the Inside Out

Core Lesson

A real glow-up doesn't start in your hair, your wardrobe, or even your highlight reel—it starts in your **soul**.

When you've been played, dumped, or used, your spirit bears the scars long after your body feels fine. Healing the inside transforms the outside.

The version of you that once begged for love, validation, or attention can rise into a version of you that **doesn't chase, doesn't settle, and doesn't compromise your worth**. This version shows up bold, radiant, and fully whole—because her foundation is built on **God's love**, not someone else's approval.

Tough Love Reality Check

- Every toxic relationship, half-love, or unfulfilling connection leaves **soul ties**—emotional and spiritual connections that linger even when the person is gone.
- Soul ties **steal clarity, drain energy, and dim your glow**.
- A glow-up without addressing the **inside** is temporary. True transformation requires discipline, healing, and intentional spiritual practices.

Real-Life Scenario

After years of chasing approval and unhealthy relationships, I realized my glow was dim because my spirit was tied up in past pain. I started **praying over past relationships**, journaling my hurt, and intentionally cultivating habits that nurtured my spirit and body.

Within months, I felt a new kind of confidence—radiant, grounded, and unapologetically whole. My glow wasn't about who noticed me—it was about who I had become in God's eyes.

Reflection Questions

1. What areas of your life need a glow-up—spirit, mind, or body?
2. Which soul ties or past wounds are draining your energy or dimming your glow?
3. How do you currently define beauty, and how can you redefine it from the inside out?
4. What habits could you incorporate to rebuild your self-worth daily?

Journaling Prompts

- List the healing habits you currently have and identify areas for improvement.
- Write about a moment you felt radiant or whole. What contributed to that feeling?
- Imagine your life six months from now if you committed to **spiritual, emotional, and physical growth**. What would it look like?

Commitment & Action Steps

1. **Daily Soul Care:** Dedicate time for prayer, journaling, or meditation each day to protect your mind and spirit.
2. **Physical Empowerment:** Move your body in ways that bring strength

and confidence, not punishment.

3. **Break Soul Ties:** Pray over past relationships and release emotional connections that aren't serving you.

4. **Create a Support System:** Surround yourself with people who encourage growth, not feed old patterns.

5. **Affirm Your Worth:** Speak daily declarations: *"I am whole. I am enough. I am God's masterpiece."*

6. **Celebrate Your Progress:** Acknowledge small wins in discipline, self-care, and emotional growth.

Commitment Challenge:

"I commit to a glow-up from the inside out. I will nurture my spirit, strengthen my mind, and empower my body, trusting God to rebuild my worth and radiance."

Accountability Challenge

- Share your commitment with a trusted friend, mentor, or small group.
- Ask them to check in weekly to discuss your progress, breakthroughs, and challenges.
- Journal accountability insights: what's working, what's challenging, and what you're learning.

Scripture Anchor

- 1 Peter 3:3-4 – *"Your beauty should not come from outward adornment... rather, it should be that of your inner self, the unfading beauty of a gentle and quiet spirit, which is of great worth in God's sight."*
- Proverbs 31:25 – *"She is clothed with strength and dignity; she can laugh at the days to come."*

Prayer & Affirmation

Prayer:

"Lord, help me glow from the inside out. Heal the wounds of my past and restore my spirit. Teach me to find beauty, worth, and confidence in You. Break the soul ties that drain me and fill me with Your peace, strength, and love. Let my glow be a reflection of Your presence in my life. Amen."

Affirmation:

I am rebuilding my spirit, mind, and body. I am radiant, disciplined, and whole. I will no longer seek validation from others because my worth comes from God. I am the prize, not the leftover, and my glow starts from the inside out.

Daily Micro-Challenges

Day 1 – Core Lesson & Reflection:

- Read the core lesson.
- Journal: Identify areas in your spirit, mind, or body that need a glow-up.

Day 2 – Tough Love Reality Check:

- Reflect on past relationships or experiences that left soul ties.
- Journal: How have these ties dimmed your glow?

Day 3 – Real-Life Scenario & Reflection:

- Read the scenario.
- Journal: Recall a moment you felt whole and radiant. What contributed to that feeling?

Day 4 – Commitment Challenge & Action Step:

- Declare your glow-up commitment aloud.
- Identify one healing habit to implement daily.

Day 5 – Accountability Challenge:

- Share your commitment with a trusted friend or mentor.
- Check-in on progress and discuss challenges.

Day 6 – Scripture Meditation:

- Meditate on 1 Peter 3:3-4 and Proverbs 31:25.
- Journal how these scriptures affirm your worth and inner beauty.

Day 7 – Reflection, Prayer & Affirmation:

- Answer reflection questions and journaling prompts.
- Pray and speak your affirmation aloud.
- Reflect on any shifts in mindset, confidence, or radiance over the week.

End-of-Week Quiz

1. True or False: My glow depends on what others think of me.
2. Identify one soul tie you need to break this week.
3. Write about a habit that will rebuild your worth daily.
4. How can redefining beauty from the inside out change your decisions and relationships?
5. Name one concrete action you will take this week to nurture your spirit, mind, or body.

End-of-Week Challenge – The Glow-Up Challenge

For the next 7 days:

- Dedicate at least 20 minutes daily to prayer, journaling, or meditation.
- Perform one physical activity that empowers your body each day.
- Speak aloud your affirmation daily: *"I am whole. I am enough. I am God's masterpiece."*
- Journal nightly about how these practices impact your confidence, decisions, and inner radiance.

Week 7 – Starving the Flesh, Feeding the Spirit

Core Lesson

Celibacy is often misunderstood. People think it's about control, restriction, or deprivation. The truth? Celibacy is about **clarity, empowerment, and alignment with God**. It's about creating a space where your spirit reigns over your flesh, and your purpose can take root.

At first, it feels impossible. Urges seem overwhelming, late-night temptations relentless, and your body cries out for satisfaction. But the more you discipline your body and guard your heart, the **weaker the urges become** and the **stronger your focus grows**.

Tough Love Reality Check

- There's a battlefield inside you—the war between **what your body wants** and **what your spirit knows is right**.
- Every suggestive message, fleeting thought, or late-night temptation is a potential distraction from the life God has for you.
- Temptation itself is not sin. Sin only occurs when you feed or act on it (Hebrews 4:15).
- Discipline is not punishment—it's **empowerment**. Each choice to guard

your heart, protect your body, and feed your spirit is a declaration of freedom over fleeting desires.

Real-Life Scenario

Late at night, scrolling through social media, I felt the familiar ache for attention and approval. Messages popped up from someone I knew wasn't right for me. My flesh screamed for connection, but my spirit whispered, *"This isn't yours to have."*

I stopped, prayed, and redirected my energy into journaling and scripture. The urge didn't vanish immediately, but over time, my clarity and self-control grew. I realized: **discipline strengthens the spirit and starves the flesh**, giving me the power to make choices aligned with God's purpose.

Reflection Questions

1. What triggers temptations for me, and how am I currently responding?
2. Where am I letting my flesh control my decisions instead of my spirit?
3. How can celibacy and discipline bring clarity and empowerment into my life?
4. What daily habits can I implement to strengthen my spirit over my flesh?

Journaling Prompts

- Write about a moment when you gave in to temptation. How did it affect your clarity, peace, and sense of purpose?
- List daily strategies to "starve the flesh," including spiritual, mental, and physical practices.
- Reflect on what freedom, power, and clarity would look like if you fully committed to discipline and celibacy.

Commitment & Action Steps

1. **Daily Word and Worship:** Begin each day in scripture and praise; grow your spirit while weakening your flesh.
2. **Guard Your Senses:** Remove triggers from social media, media, and conversations that stimulate temptation.
3. **Accountability Partner:** Engage someone trustworthy to check in, pray with you, and hold you accountable.
4. **Physical Outlets:** Exercise, dance, or channel energy positively to refocus your body and mind.
5. **Prayer as Armor:** Counter temptation with scripture, worship, and spoken declarations: *"I honor my body. I choose purity. I am a temple of God."*
6. **Intimacy with God:** Make daily time with Him non-negotiable; the closer you are to His heart, the easier it is to resist destruction.

Commitment Challenge:
"I commit to starving my flesh and feeding my spirit daily. I will guard my heart, discipline my body, and prioritize God's presence above all else."

Accountability Challenge

- Share your commitment with a trusted friend, mentor, or small group.
- Check in weekly about progress, struggles, and victories.
- Journal accountability insights: what's working, what's challenging, and what you're learning.

Scripture Anchor

- Hebrews 4:15 – *"For we do not have a high priest who is unable to empathize with our weaknesses, but we have one who has been tempted in every way, just as we are—yet he did not sin."*
- 1 Corinthians 9:27 – *"But I discipline my body and keep it under control, lest*

after preaching to others I myself should be disqualified."

Prayer & Affirmation

Prayer:

"Lord, make me whole, not desperate. Help me master my flesh before it masters me. Give me clarity, strength, and discipline to guard my heart, my mind, and my body. Teach me to feed my spirit instead of my desires. Let my focus remain on You, and let my life reflect Your purpose and glory. Amen."

Affirmation:

I am not a slave to desire. I am disciplined, empowered, and focused. My body, my heart, and my mind honor God. I feed my spirit, not my flesh, and I walk in clarity, freedom, and purpose.

Daily Micro-Challenges

Day 1 – Core Lesson & Reflection:

- Read the core lesson.
- Journal: Identify one temptation that consistently challenges your focus.

Day 2 – Tough Love Reality Check:

- Reflect on times when flesh-controlled decisions caused confusion or pain.
- Journal: What pattern do you need to break?

Day 3 – Real-Life Scenario & Reflection:

- Read the scenario.
- Journal: How did redirecting energy or prayer strengthen your clarity?

Day 4 – Commitment Challenge & Action Step:

- Declare your commitment aloud.
- Take one concrete step today to guard your senses or discipline your body.

Day 5 – Accountability Challenge:

- Share your commitment with an accountability partner.
- Check in on progress and challenges.

Day 6 – Scripture Meditation:

- Meditate on Hebrews 4:15 and 1 Corinthians 9:27.
- Journal how these scriptures empower your discipline and clarity.

Day 7 – Reflection, Prayer & Affirmation:

- Complete reflection questions and journaling prompts.
- Pray and speak your affirmation aloud.
- Reflect on any changes in clarity, discipline, or spiritual alignment.

End-of-Week Quiz

1. True or False: Temptation itself is sin.
2. Name one trigger you need to guard against this week.
3. List one physical, one mental, and one spiritual strategy to feed your spirit daily.
4. How does discipline over the flesh empower your purpose?
5. What action will you take this week to strengthen your clarity and self-control?

End-of-Week Challenge – The Spirit-Focused Challenge

For the next 7 days:

- Begin each day with scripture, prayer, and worship.
- Remove or limit at least one trigger from your environment that tempts your flesh.
- Engage in one physical outlet that strengthens your body and focus.
- Speak your affirmation aloud daily: *"I am disciplined, empowered, and focused. I feed my spirit, not my flesh."*
- Journal nightly about victories, challenges, and insights gained.

Week 8 – Learning How to Love Being Alone

Core Lesson

Being alone is **not the same as being lonely**. For many of us, especially those who have never truly experienced solitude, the two are often confused.

Alone is power. Alone is freedom. Alone is where God meets you in ways the noise of the world never can. In your single season, learning to enjoy your own company cultivates peace, clarity, and spiritual growth.

The Difference Between Lonely and Alone:

- **Lonely:** An ache for something outside of you to fill the emptiness. Desperate, incomplete, restless.
- **Alone:** A space to reconnect with yourself, explore your heart, and hear God's voice without distraction. Alone is intentional, healing, and sacred.

The power of being alone comes from **cultivating joy, creating sacred space, and choosing silence over toxic noise**. Your spirit can grow, clarity emerges, and God speaks most clearly in solitude.

Tough Love Reality Check

- Many confuse being alone with being lonely. Avoiding solitude often leads to unhealthy dependence on others for validation.
- Solitude isn't a punishment—it's preparation. Alone time is **opportunity for spiritual growth, emotional healing, and self-discovery**.
- You cannot thrive in relationships or life fully until you learn to be at peace with your own company.

Real-Life Scenario

I remember when I first experienced true solitude in my single season. For years, I had always been surrounded—siblings, friends, children, relationships. Alone felt scary and uncomfortable. I felt unwanted, useless, and uncertain of my worth.

But as I began to embrace intentional alone-time, I noticed a shift. I created a sanctuary in my space, practiced quiet reflection, and let God speak to my heart. Slowly, the ache of loneliness transformed into joy, clarity, and freedom. Alone was no longer a threat—it was a gift.

Reflection Questions

1. What does your current experience of solitude reveal about your relationship with yourself?
2. Where do you confuse loneliness with being alone?
3. How can you turn your alone-time into a sacred space for healing, joy, and clarity?
4. What activities or habits can you implement to find peace and pleasure in your own company?

Journaling Prompts

- Write about a moment when you truly felt alone. How did it feel? How did your spirit respond?
- List three ways you can cultivate joy and peace in your own space starting today.
- Reflect on your fears of being alone. How might these fears be hiding opportunities for freedom and growth?

Commitment & Action Steps

1. **Start Small:** Begin with intentional alone-time, even 15 minutes a day, for reflection and prayer.
2. **Create a Routine:** Dedicate regular time for journaling, prayer, or meditation to anchor your day.
3. **Engage Your Senses:** Light candles, play soft music, brew tea—make your space inviting and joyful.
4. **Turn to God:** Ask Him to reveal His presence, speak to your heart, and show you the value of solitude.
5. **Celebrate Wins:** Notice small achievements and ways your spirit grows during these moments.

Commitment Challenge:

"I commit to embracing intentional alone-time, finding joy, peace, and purpose in my own company. I will use solitude as a sacred space to connect with God and grow in my worth."

Accountability Challenge

- Share your commitment with a trusted friend or mentor.
- Ask them to check in weekly about your progress in embracing solitude.
- Journal insights: what's working, what's challenging, and what you're discovering about yourself and God.

Scripture Anchor

- Psalm 46:10 – *"Be still, and know that I am God."*
- Isaiah 30:15 – *"In repentance and rest is your salvation, in quietness and trust is your strength."*

Prayer & Affirmation

Prayer:

"Lord, teach me to love being alone. Help me embrace solitude without fear or despair. Show me how to create joy, peace, and purpose in my own space. Let Your voice be loudest in the quiet moments, and let Your presence fill the places where I feel empty. Amen."

Affirmation:

I am not lonely; I am powerful. I am whole, radiant, and complete in my own company. Alone is my sanctuary, my space to grow, to hear God, and to thrive. I embrace solitude as a season of preparation, peace, and self-discovery.

Daily Micro-Challenges

Day 1 – Core Lesson & Reflection:

- Read the core lesson.
- Journal: Identify one fear you have about being alone.

Day 2 – Tough Love Reality Check:

- Reflect on how avoiding alone-time has affected your growth or self-discovery.
- Journal: How can solitude benefit your spiritual and emotional life?

Day 3 – Real-Life Scenario & Reflection:

- Read the scenario.
- Journal: How might you create a sacred space for yourself this week?

Day 4 – Commitment Challenge & Action Step:

- Declare your commitment aloud.
- Take one action today to create a peaceful, joyful, and intentional alone-time.

Day 5 – Accountability Challenge:

- Share your commitment with a mentor, friend, or small group.
- Check in on progress and challenges.

Day 6 – Scripture Meditation:

- Meditate on Psalm 46:10 and Isaiah 30:15.
- Journal how these verses help you embrace and find peace in solitude.

Day 7 – Reflection, Prayer & Affirmation:

- Complete reflection questions and journaling prompts.
- Pray and speak your affirmation aloud.
- Reflect on changes in mindset, peace, or connection with God.

End-of-Week Quiz

1. True or False: Being alone is the same as being lonely.
2. List two ways you can intentionally create joy and peace in your own space.
3. How does solitude strengthen your relationship with God?
4. Name one fear you have about being alone and how you can confront it.
5. What action will you take this week to embrace alone-time as sacred?

End-of-Week Challenge – The Solitude Challenge

For the next 7 days:

- Dedicate at least 15 minutes daily to intentional alone-time.
- Engage in one activity that nurtures your spirit—prayer, journaling, meditation, or creativity.
- Remove distractions and toxic noise during this time.
- Celebrate your presence, progress, and the clarity gained.
- Journal nightly about insights, victories, and spiritual growth discovered in solitude.

III

Part Three: Thriving on Purpose

Week 9 – Boundaries That Save Your Life

Core Lesson

B oundaries are **not optional—they are essential**. Every moment you allow someone to overstep, compromise, or disrespect your space chips away at your peace, your joy, and your self-worth.

Too often, we've been conditioned to believe: "Whatever feels good, go for it. Just take it." But chasing fleeting pleasure comes at a cost. **Boundaries aren't about restriction—they are about protection.** They are your armor, your power, and your declaration of worth.

Stop Letting Him "Just Come Over to Chill":

- Saying yes because it's easier than saying no chips away at your peace.
- Saying yes out of guilt or fear of conflict compromises your standards.
- Respect starts with you. If you don't honor your standards, no one else will.

Protect Your Peace and Honor Your Heart and Body:

- **Physical boundaries:** Protect your body from casual encounters, empty affection, or half-hearted attention.
- **Emotional boundaries:** Guard your feelings from those who dismiss, ignore, or undervalue them.
- **Spiritual boundaries:** Shield your spirit from influences that distract

53

you from God's plan.

Real-Life Scenario

I remember letting someone "just come over" because I didn't want to hurt their feelings. By the time they left, I felt drained, frustrated, and a little empty. That night, I realized my peace was non-negotiable. I committed to only allowing people into my life who **respected my boundaries, my time, and my heart**. Implementing boundaries changed everything.

Reflection Questions

1. Where have you allowed others to overstep your boundaries?
2. How has saying "yes" too often cost you your peace or self-respect?
3. Which areas of your life need stricter boundaries—physical, emotional, or spiritual?
4. How will honoring your boundaries change your relationships and personal growth?

Journaling Prompts

- List the top three boundaries you need to implement in your life right now.
- Write about a time you said yes when you should have said no. How did it affect your peace?
- Visualize your life after fully honoring your heart, body, and spirit. What does it look like?

Practical Steps to Establish and Protect Boundaries

1. **Identify Your Standards:** Know what is non-negotiable for your body, heart, and mind.
2. **Communicate Clearly:** Speak your boundaries assertively—don't hint,

justify, or apologize.

3. **Enforce Them:** If someone violates your boundaries, take immediate action—block numbers, step away, or remove yourself from the situation.

4. **Stay Accountable:** Share your boundaries with trusted friends or mentors who can support you.

5. **Trust God's Timing:** Wait for people who honor your standards and encourage your growth. The right person will respect your boundaries naturally.

Prayer & Declaration

Prayer:

"Lord, give me the courage to set boundaries that protect my heart, my body, and my peace. Help me say no without guilt, enforce my standards, and honor the sacredness of what You have entrusted to me. Surround me with people who uplift, encourage, and respect me. Amen."

Declaration:

My body and my heart are sacred. I will not compromise my peace for anyone. I am worthy of respect, love, and devotion. I will set boundaries without guilt and only allow people into my life who honor my standards and encourage my growth.

Daily Micro-Challenges

Day 1 – Core Lesson & Reflection:

- Read the core lesson.
- Journal: Identify one area where your boundaries are weak and why.

Day 2 – Tough Love Reality Check:

- Reflect on the cost of saying "yes" too often.

- Journal: How has this affected your peace and self-respect?

Day 3 – Real-Life Scenario & Reflection:

- Read the scenario.
- Journal: How can you enforce your boundaries starting today?

Day 4 – Commitment Challenge & Action Step:

- Declare your commitment aloud: "I will protect my peace and honor my heart."
- Take one immediate action to strengthen a boundary (block a number, say no, or step away from a situation).

Day 5 – Accountability Challenge:

- Share your commitment with a trusted friend or mentor.
- Ask them to check in weekly to support your boundary enforcement.

Day 6 – Scripture Meditation:

- Meditate on Proverbs 4:23 – *"Above all else, guard your heart, for everything you do flows from it."*
- Journal how this verse motivates you to honor your boundaries.

Day 7 – Reflection, Prayer & Affirmation:

- Complete reflection questions and journaling prompts.
- Pray and speak your declaration aloud.
- Reflect on how enforcing boundaries impacts your peace, confidence, and clarity.

End-of-Week Quiz

1. True or False: Boundaries are optional in healthy relationships.
2. List two areas in your life where stronger boundaries are needed.
3. How has saying "yes" too often affected your growth and peace?
4. Name one physical, emotional, or spiritual boundary you will enforce this week.
5. What action will you take to honor your heart, body, and spirit?

End-of-Week Challenge – The Boundaries Challenge

For the next 7 days:

- Identify one area each day to enforce a boundary.
- Actively remove or distance yourself from influences that compromise your peace.
- Reflect daily in your journal about how maintaining boundaries affects your clarity, confidence, and spiritual growth.
- Celebrate small victories when you honor yourself and protect your heart, body, and spirit.

Week 10 – The Glow-Up Mindset

Core Lesson

Choosing yourself is revolutionary. In a world that constantly pressures you to seek validation from others, choosing yourself boldly, unapologetically, and consistently is magnetic. It signals to the world—and to the right people—that you are **whole, confident, and untouchable by temporary approval.**

Thriving while single isn't about waiting for someone to complete you. It's about **being complete in yourself**, living in joy, and cultivating a glow that nobody—not circumstances, not people, not situations—can dim.

No Apologies for Choosing Yourself:

- Prioritize your heart, mind, body, and spirit.
- Say yes to God's purpose, even if it means saying no to distractions, toxic people, or half-hearted love.
- Celebrate your wins: Big or small, acknowledge progress without shame.
- Protect your energy: Don't apologize for prioritizing your peace.
- Live unapologetically: Your joy, growth, and clarity are non-negotiable.

Thriving Single Makes You Magnetic:

- Confidence grows from clarity: Knowing who you are in God's eyes gives you unshakeable self-assurance.

- Joy is contagious: Fulfillment attracts others to your energy naturally.
- Boundaries amplify your glow: Standing firm in your standards signals that you value yourself—and so will others.

Becoming Whole: The Glow Nobody Can Dim

A true glow-up starts internally. Wholeness is:

- Security in your identity and value.
- Freedom from seeking external validation to feel worthy.
- Confidence rooted in God's love and purpose for your life.

Reflection Questions

1. In what ways are you currently choosing yourself—or not choosing yourself?
2. How does thriving single make you feel more confident and empowered?
3. What aspects of your life need a glow-up that doesn't rely on external validation?
4. How can you embody wholeness daily so your glow is untouchable?

Journaling Prompts

- Write about a moment when you felt fully radiant and confident without needing anyone's approval.
- List three ways you can choose yourself today—emotionally, spiritually, or physically.
- Reflect on how thriving in your singleness can attract people who align with your values and purpose.

Practical Steps to Cultivate the Glow-Up Mindset

1. **Daily Affirmations:** Speak life over yourself each morning: *"I am whole. I am enough. I am radiant in God's love."*
2. **Intentional Joy:** Schedule activities that bring pleasure, growth, and peace without relying on anyone else.
3. **Protect Your Peace:** Maintain boundaries with people and situations that drain or distract you.
4. **Invest in You:** Commit to spiritual, emotional, and physical growth. Your glow comes from holistic alignment with God.
5. **Celebrate Wholeness:** Recognize milestones in independence, growth, and self-discovery.

Prayer & Declaration

Prayer:

"God, help me walk boldly in my worth. Teach me to thrive in my singleness, to embrace my wholeness, and to radiate confidence without apology. Let my joy, peace, and purpose shine, and attract what aligns with Your will for my life. Amen."

Declaration:

I choose myself unapologetically. I am whole, radiant, and confident. My glow comes from within, and nobody can dim it. I live in joy, clarity, and purpose, and I attract only what aligns with God's plan for me.

Daily Micro-Challenges

Day 1 – Core Lesson & Reflection:

- Read the core lesson.
- Journal: Identify one area where you need to choose yourself more intentionally.

Day 2 – Magnetic Thriving:

- Reflect on how thriving single makes you more confident.
- Journal: How can your energy attract people who align with your values?

Day 3 – Wholeness Check:

- Write down ways your glow depends on internal growth rather than external validation.
- Journal: How can you nurture each area (spirit, mind, body) this week?

Day 4 – Affirmation Practice:

- Speak your affirmation aloud multiple times today.
- Journal: How does declaring your worth affect your confidence?

Day 5 – Intentional Joy:

- Plan one activity today that brings you joy independent of anyone else.
- Journal: How does it feel to prioritize your happiness?

Day 6 – Protect & Reflect:

- Identify one boundary to enforce this week to safeguard your peace.
- Journal: How will this boundary strengthen your glow?

Day 7 – Celebration & Declaration:

- Reflect on the week's growth.
- Speak your declaration aloud and journal the ways you embody wholeness.

End-of-Week Quiz

1. True or False: Thriving single is about waiting for someone to complete you.
2. List two ways choosing yourself can make you magnetic.
3. How does internal wholeness affect your glow?
4. Name one habit to cultivate joy independently this week.
5. What affirmation will you speak daily to reinforce your worth?

End-of-Week Challenge – The Glow-Up Challenge

For the next 7 days:

- Commit to one intentional act each day that prioritizes your growth, joy, and peace.
- Journal daily about how these actions reinforce your glow-up mindset.
- At the end of the week, reflect on how your inner confidence and wholeness have shifted your perspective and energy.

Week 11 – If Love Shows Up, Fine. If Not, Still Fine

Core Lesson

L ove will show up when it's meant to—but only after you've learned to thrive in your own completeness. Too many women fall into the trap of seeking someone to complete them, fill their gaps, or validate their worth. That's where **counterfeit love thrives**.

When you are whole, love doesn't define you—it **complements you**.

Recognizing the Real Thing vs. the Counterfeit:

Counterfeit Love:

- Comes with inconsistencies—words don't match actions.
- Feels addictive but leaves emptiness in its wake.
- Is often convenient rather than committed.
- Pressures you to compromise your boundaries.
- Leaves you doubting your worth or feeling incomplete.

Real Love:

- Shows up with integrity, consistency, and respect.
- Enhances your life rather than filling voids.
- Encourages growth, discipline, and spiritual alignment.

- Supports your boundaries and honors your heart and body.
- Complements your wholeness, rather than completing you.

Scenario Example:

You've been texting a guy for months. He's charming, attentive late at night, but never makes meaningful plans. He says, "I like you, but I'm not ready." That's a counterfeit—he wants connection without commitment.

Contrast that with a man who consistently shows up, respects your space, celebrates your goals, and values your heart. That is **real love**—love that complements, not confines.

Living Fully While Waiting

Waiting is not passive. Thriving while single is **active preparation**:

- Grow spiritually, emotionally, and physically.
- Build your career, friendships, and passions.
- Cultivate joy, self-respect, and personal boundaries.
- Prepare to link up with someone who matches your wholeness, not your gaps.

Choosing Partnership, Not Bondage:

- A healthy relationship enhances life; it does not enslave you to someone else's whims or insecurities.
- Whole people attract whole love.
- You are complete and content on your own.
- Seek companionship that complements your life, not completes it.
- Understand that love is a choice, not a necessity to validate your existence.

Reflection Questions

1. How can you recognize counterfeit love before it steals your peace?
2. In what ways are you thriving while single, independent of a partner?
3. What does a relationship that complements your wholeness look like?
4. How would your life change if you truly lived fully instead of "waiting" for someone else?

Journaling Prompts

- List the qualities that distinguish counterfeit love from real love based on your experiences.
- Write about ways you are currently thriving and building wholeness while single.
- Imagine your life six months or a year from now as a single, thriving woman. How do you feel, and what kind of love would fit seamlessly into your life?

Practical Steps to Attract Whole Love While Thriving Single

1. **Set Non-Negotiables:** Know your values, deal-breakers, and what love should feel like.
2. **Guard Your Heart:** Only invest in relationships that honor your boundaries and encourage growth.
3. **Invest in Wholeness:** Prioritize personal growth, spiritual depth, and emotional healing.
4. **Observe Actions, Not Words:** Consistency, respect, and integrity reveal the real thing.
5. **Celebrate Your Life Now:** Focus on joy, purpose, and fulfillment today, rather than depending on tomorrow's romance.

Prayer & Declaration

Prayer:

"Lord, help me recognize real love and avoid counterfeit distractions. Teach me to thrive fully while single and cultivate wholeness that attracts the right partner. Let my joy, purpose, and peace not depend on another, but be rooted in You. Amen."

Declaration:

I am whole, radiant, and thriving. I attract only love that complements my wholeness, not completes it. I will not settle for counterfeit or convenience. I choose joy, growth, and purpose while single, trusting God to bring the right partner at the right time.

Daily Micro-Challenges

Day 1 – Recognizing Counterfeit vs. Real Love:

- Journal about past experiences with love that didn't honor your wholeness.
- Identify red flags for counterfeit love.

Day 2 – Thriving Single:

- List 3 ways you are thriving spiritually, emotionally, or physically while single.

Day 3 – Wholeness Reflection:

- Reflect on areas of your life where you feel complete.
- Journal how a partner could complement, not complete, this wholeness.

Day 4 – Non-Negotiables:

- Write down your top 5 values and deal-breakers in a partner.
- Visualize the kind of love that matches your standards.

Day 5 – Guarding Your Heart:

- Identify one relationship or pattern to step back from that compromises your peace.
- Journal about how enforcing this boundary strengthens your glow.

Day 6 – Observing Actions:

- Reflect on a current or past connection. Are their actions aligned with their words?
- Journal what consistency would look like in a real relationship.

Day 7 – Celebrating Your Life:

- List 5 ways you are thriving today as a single woman.
- Speak your declaration aloud and visualize attracting love that complements your wholeness.

End-of-Week Quiz

1. True or False: Love should complete you to make you whole.
2. Name two qualities that distinguish real love from counterfeit love.
3. List three ways you can thrive while single.
4. What is one non-negotiable you will enforce in future relationships?
5. How can observing actions, not words, help you recognize real love?

End-of-Week Challenge – Whole Love Challenge

- This week, focus on **thriving fully in your wholeness**.
- Journal daily about your spiritual, emotional, and physical growth.
- At the end of the week, reflect on how your clarity, joy, and boundaries strengthen your readiness for a partner who complements your life.

Week 12 – Choosing Me, Every Day

Core Lesson

Singleness is not a curse—it is a **calling season**, a sacred time where God prepares, shapes, and strengthens you for the life He has designed. This season is not about lack—it's about **growth, discovery, and empowerment**.

Thriving single is **preparation, power, and purpose**. It is the time to learn who you are when no one else is watching, to cultivate joy that isn't dependent on a partner, and to embrace wholeness as your ultimate superpower.

Choosing you is not a one-time decision.

It is a **daily declaration**, a conscious act of self-love, spiritual alignment, and empowerment. Every day you choose yourself, you:

- Reinforce your worth.
- Protect your peace.
- Cultivate a glow that cannot be dimmed.

To Every Woman Walking This Road

I see you. I see the nights of tears, the moments of doubt, the times you felt unseen, used, or overlooked. I see your courage, resilience, and determination to rise above.

- You are not broken—you are becoming.
- You are not incomplete—you are whole.
- Your singleness is your classroom, your preparation, and your launchpad for a life of purpose and power.

This journey isn't easy, but it **is worth it**. Each day you choose yourself, you choose freedom. Each day you honor your boundaries, your heart, and your spirit, you choose God's design over the world's lies. Each day you walk boldly in your worth, you choose the glow that radiates from the inside out.

Reflection Questions

1. How can I honor myself daily during this season of singleness?
2. What boundaries, habits, or practices reinforce my peace and wholeness?
3. In what ways have I grown spiritually, emotionally, and physically while being single?
4. How can I embrace joy, clarity, and empowerment independent of a partner?

Journaling Prompts

- Write about a moment recently when you chose yourself over temporary validation or external approval. How did it feel?
- List three ways you can honor your worth and protect your peace every day.
- Reflect on the ways God is shaping you in this season and how your wholeness is becoming your superpower.

Practical Steps to Embrace Daily Self-Choice

1. **Start Each Day Intentionally:** Begin with prayer, reflection, or affirmation of your worth.
2. **Honor Your Boundaries:** Protect your heart, body, and spirit from

anything or anyone that diminishes your peace.

3. **Prioritize Growth:** Invest in spiritual, emotional, and physical practices that reinforce your wholeness.
4. **Celebrate Wins:** Acknowledge small victories in self-care, discipline, and personal empowerment.
5. **Radiate Your Glow:** Let your inner strength, joy, and confidence shine outward, independent of external validation.

Daily Prayer

"Lord, help every woman walking this season of singleness to see her value through Your eyes. Teach us to choose ourselves daily, to honor our hearts, protect our peace, and embrace the wholeness You've given us. Help us walk boldly in our purpose, thrive in our solitude, and trust that every step of this season is shaping us into the women You created us to be. Let our wholeness be our superpower, and let our lives reflect Your glory in every choice we make. Amen."

Daily Affirmation

I CHOOSE ME!

Today, I honor my worth, protect my peace, and embrace my wholeness. I am enough, I am radiant, and I am complete. I choose growth, I choose joy, I choose God's purpose for my life. I choose me—**every single day**.

Daily Micro-Challenges

Day 1 – Morning Intention:

- Begin your day with the affirmation: *"I choose me today."*
- Journal one area you will honor yourself.

Day 2 – Boundary Check:

- Identify one area where you may be compromising your peace.
- Take action to reinforce your boundaries.

Day 3 – Celebrate Growth:

- Reflect on three ways you've grown this season of singleness.
- Journal how that growth impacts your wholeness.

Day 4 – Joy Practice:

- Do one activity purely for your joy—without needing approval or attention from anyone else.

Day 5 – Spiritual Alignment:

- Spend intentional time in prayer, meditation, or worship.
- Focus on receiving God's affirmation of your worth.

Day 6 – Radiate Your Glow:

- Identify ways your inner glow shows in your daily life.
- Compliment yourself on at least one personal strength or achievement.

Day 7 – Reflection & Celebration:

- Reflect on the week and journal your biggest wins in self-love, boundaries, and empowerment.

Speak your affirmation aloud and embrace your daily choice to put yourself first.

POWERFUL CLOSING REMINDER

You are enough. You are radiant. You are whole.
Every choice you make to honor yourself, guard your heart,
and walk in purpose strengthens the glow that comes from within.
Your **wholeness is your superpower**
—let it guide you, protect you, and radiate into every area of your life.
Keep choosing YOU, every single day.
With love, faith, and encouragement,

Chanita R. Ramsey

End-of-Book Declaration

I am whole, radiant, and empowered.
I honor my worth, protect my peace, and embrace the wholeness God has
given me.
I choose me every single day, thriving in purpose, joy, and clarity.
My glow is from the inside out, and nobody can dim it.

AUTHOR'S NOTE

Dear Reader,

Congratulations! You've taken intentional steps toward wholeness, self-love, and spiritual alignment. Completing this workbook is **not the end**—it's the beginning of a life where you thrive, protect your peace, and walk boldly in God's purpose.

You are not defined by your past or your circumstances. You are defined by your **daily choices**—to honor yourself, guard your heart, and cultivate your wholeness. Every step matters.

NEXT STEPS: KEEP THRIVING

1. Daily Wholeness Declaration

Speak life over yourself each morning.

"I am whole. I am enough. I walk in God's purpose."

"I protect my peace, honor my heart, and choose growth."

"I am radiant, disciplined, and empowered from the inside out."

My Daily Declaration:

2. One Boundary to Protect Your Peace

Identify one area in your life that needs a boundary.

- **Boundary:** _____
- **Action to enforce it:** _____

3. Growth Goal

- **Pick one meaningful step to grow spiritually, emotionally, or physically in the next 7 days.**
- **Growth Step:** _____
- **How I'll track progress:** _____

4. Celebrate Yourself

Acknowledge your wins—big or small.

1.
2.
3.
4.
5.
6.

5. Final Reflection

At the end of the week, reflect on your journey. Answer freely:

- How has choosing yourself, protecting your peace, and investing in your wholeness changed my energy and perspective?